Nature Craft

Fiona Hayes

Quarto is the authority on a wide range of topics.

Quarto educates, entertains and enriches the lives of
our readers—enthusiasts and lovers of hands-on living.

www.quartoknows.com

Design and Editorial: Calcium Creative Ltd
Photography: Michael Wicks
Illustration: Tom Connell
With thanks to our wonderful models Thomas and Lily

This edition first published in 2018 by QEB Publishing,
an imprint of The Quarto Group.
6 Orchard Road, Suite 100
Lake Forest, CA 92630
T: +1 949 380 7510
F: +1 949 380 7575
www.QuartoKnows.com

A CIP record for this book is available from the
Library of Congress.

ISBN: 978-1-68297-372-1

Manufactured in
Dongguan, China TL042018

9 8 7 6 5 4 3 2 1

MIX
Paper from
responsible sources
FSC® C104723
FSC
www.fsc.org

Nature Craft

Fiona Hayes

QEB

Contents

Introduction

The projects in this book use a variety of natural materials and a few simple items that you may have at home. Most of the natural materials are easy to find if you know where and when to look.

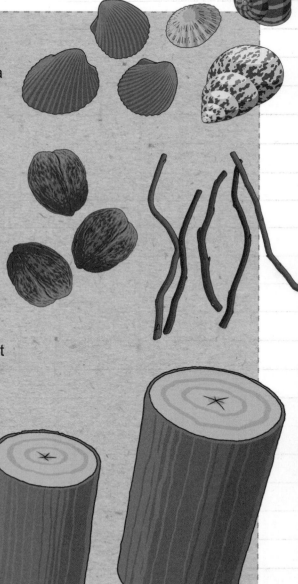

Finding Natural Materials

Next time you are outside, stop and take a look at the nature around you. You might see trees, bushes, grassland, flowerbeds, fields, or gardens. Each of these places is home to natural materials.

- Carry a bag with you when you go out to collect your finds.

- Look up to see the types of trees that are growing. Do they have acorns or pine cones? Do they have brightly colored leaves? Look around for these fallen treasures.

- Collect a mixture of straight sticks, bent sticks, narrow sticks, and thick sticks.

- Try to find a variety of seed pods.

- Search in soil for empty snail shells.

- Hunt on the beach for empty shells and interesting pebbles.

When to Look?

You can find interesting things throughout the year, but especially in fall. It is a great time of year to collect sticks, leaves, and seeds. Leaves change color and fall to the ground. Seed pods are blown from trees in strong winds.

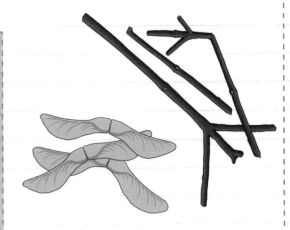

Preparing Natural Materials

Most of your finds, such as pebbles, sticks, shells, and seed pods, can be cleaned using dishwashing soap and warm water. Gently sponge clean your items with warm, soapy water. Leave the materials to dry fully before you begin your project. Always wash your hands after handling your finds.

Basic Equipment

There are detailed lists of equipment for each project. Most projects will also use some of the following equipment:

- White glue or a cool-melt glue gun
- Paint
- Paint brushes
- Felt-tip pens
- Pencils
- Scissors
- Ruler

Bird Mask

At the end of summer, birds lose their feathers and then grow new ones, but do not collect these feathers for your mask.

1

Use the template on page 68 to draw a mask shape onto cardstock and cut it out. Use the tip of a pencil to make a hole for your scissors, then cut out two holes for the eyes. Make one small hole on each side of the mask.

2

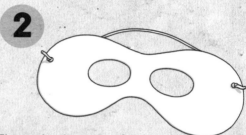

Thread a length of thin elastic through each hole. Tie a knot in each end.

3

Glue long feathers to the front of the top of the mask.

4

Add smaller feathers in front of the long ones.

8

5

Cut out small triangles from different colored felt.

6

Glue the felt triangles around the edge of the mask. Leave a space where your nose will go.

7

Continue gluing on the triangles, overlapping them until you have covered the mask.

8

Fold a piece of yellow cardstock in half. Cut out a triangle. Open out to make the beak.

9

Glue the edges of the beak onto the mask. Put on your mask and start flapping!

Snails

1

Paint some of the shells and leave some natural.

2

Roll a piece of modeling clay into a sausage shape. Bend one end of the shape up slightly. This will be the head. Push two sticks into the head. Make more bodies and bend some so they can hang over an edge. Let the clay dry.

3

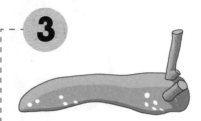

Paint the snail bodies.

4

Glue a pair of googly eyes to the tops of the sticks. Glue the shells to the bodies.

5

Find a flower pot for your snails to climb over.

Flowers

1

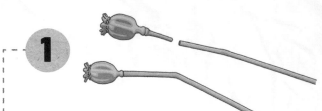

You will need

Green paint
Dried poppy seed heads
Green bendy straws
Scrap paper
Crepe paper

Cut the stems of the poppy seed heads short. Paint some of them green. Glue them into the end of the bendy green straws.

2

Trace the petal template on page 69 onto scrap paper. Cut it out. Cut a strip of crepe paper just wider than the petal template.

3

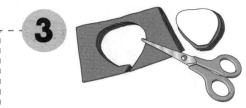

Fold the strip of crepe paper into five equal sections. Place the template on top and draw around it. Cut out all the petals at once.

4

Glue the narrow end of a petal around the top of a straw. Continue with the other four petals. Overlap each petal with the previous one by about half its width.

5

Make lots of different colored flowers so you have a whole bunch.

Bird's Nest

Birds build nests from sticks, grasses, leaves, and even mud, stones, and saliva!

1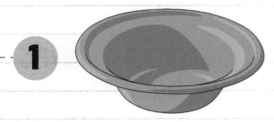

Paint a paper bowl light brown.

2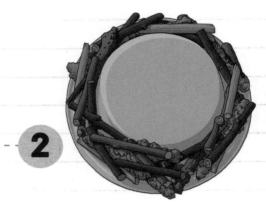

When it is dry, turn your bowl over. Glue short pieces of twig around the sides. Make them overlap each other.

3

Turn your bowl right side up. Glue more twigs around the rim.

4

Push some small feathers between the twigs to complete your nest.

Coral Reef and Fish

1

Glue an acorn cup to each pine cone. Paint the cone and acorn cup or leave natural.

2

Glue a shell to each side and the end of each cone. Push them between the cone scales.

3

For each fish, paint two acorn cups white. Add a black dot to each one. Glue them onto the cone. Tie string around the cone and then tie into a loop.

4

Paint a branch orange to make it look like coral. Draw on markings in felt-tip pen. Hang your fish on the piece of coral.

Owls

Pine cones can be male or female. Female pine cones contain seeds. The seeds fall to the ground with the cone and may grow into a new tree.

1

Paint some of the pine cones and leave others unpainted.

2

For each cone, cut a diamond from felt. Make it about the same length as the cone.

3

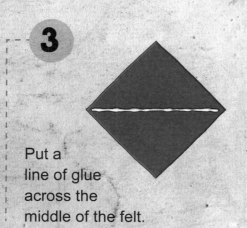

Put a line of glue across the middle of the felt.

4

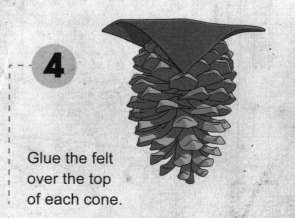

Glue the felt over the top of each cone.

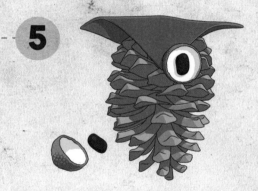

5

For each cone, paint the insides of two acorn cups white. Glue a dried bean into each one. Stick them to the front of the cone.

6

For each owl, cut out a beak from yellow felt and glue in place.

7

Sit the owls on a branch. If they fall off, attach them with adhesive putty.

Handy Hint
Large owls may need googly eyes instead of acorn and bean eyes.

HOOT
HOOT

Bunny

Pine cones come in lots of different sizes and shapes. Make sure you dry them before you use them.

1

Paint the pine cone gray (or leave unpainted).

2

Glue a pair of mussel shells to the top of the cone. Try to push the pointed end of the shells between the scales of the cone. Make sure the insides of the shells are facing forward.

3

Paint the outside of another pair of mussel shells the same gray as the bunny's body. Glue them to the bottom of the cone for the bunny's feet.

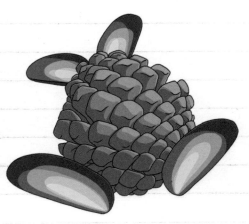

4 Draw on some toes with a black pen.

5 Glue a pair of googly eyes to the front.

6 Glue on a small pink pompom nose and a white pompom tail.

Handy Hint
Look under conifer trees for pine cones. You will be most likely to find them in late fall and early winter.

HOP! HOP!

Tortoise

1

Paint a foam ball and four cockle shells green.

2

Turn the coconut shell over. Glue the cockle shells to the edge of the coconut shell to make the feet.

3

Turn the coconut shell back up the right way. Glue on the foam ball for the head.

4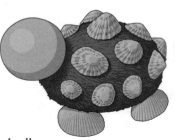

Glue limpet shells over the coconut shell.

5

For the eyes, paint two acorn cups green. Add a big black dot and a smaller white dot to each cup.

6

Glue the eyes to the head. Add yellow spots and a smile.

Star

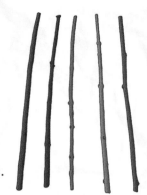

1
Cut five sticks to the same length.

You will need

Five long, narrow sticks

Five rubber bands

Colored yarn

2
Make them into a "W" shape. Wrap a rubber band around the sticks that cross over each other.

3
Take the two outer sticks and pull them toward each other so that they cross over.

4
Put the fifth stick across the top to join the two stick ends. Wrap rubber bands around both ends of this stick. Tie yarn around the sticks that cross over each other in the middle of the star to strengthen it.

5
Wrap yarn around the star's points to decorate it.

Dragonflies

You can find the helicopter seeds to make your dragonflies' wings in late summer and fall.

You will need

Green and blue paint
Thin sticks
Colored raffia
Helicopter seeds
Blue and brown felt
Googly eyes
Bamboo cane or long, straight stick
Corrugated cardboard
Thick cardstock

1

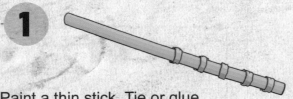

Paint a thin stick. Tie or glue some raffia around it to create a stripy body for the dragonfly.

2

Cut out a shape from the felt that looks a bit like a number 8. Make sure it is slightly larger than the googly eyes. Glue the eyes to the felt.

3

Glue the eyes to the head of your dragonfly.

4

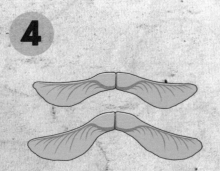

Take two pairs of helicopter seeds for the wings. Either leave them natural colored or paint them.

5

Glue the wings to the body so they cross over. Make some more dragonflies with different colored stripes.

6

For the bulrush stem, paint a bamboo cane or long, straight stick green. Cut a piece of corrugated cardboard that is about one-third the length of the stick. Glue the cardboard around the stick, leaving a small section of stick poking out from the top.

7

Cut a piece of brown felt that is slightly longer than the corrugated cardboard. Glue this around the cardboard. Make sure you glue the excess felt to the top and bottom of the roll.

8

Cut out some leaves from thick cardstock and paint them green. Glue the leaves to the bulrush stem.

9

Now glue the dragonflies onto the bulrushes.

21

Squirrel

Squirrels eat almost any kind of nut, but especially like acorns and walnuts.

1

Paint a pine cone brown. Ask an adult to help cut two short thick sticks. Paint them brown.

2

Glue the sticks to the bottom sides of the cone. A cool melt gun works well for this.

3

Paint the foam egg brown. Glue it to the top of the cone.

Handy Hint

Look for dried grasses on footpaths and the outer edges of fields. Do not pick grasses growing as crops in farmers' fields.

4

Cut out a slight curve from thick cardstock for the tail. Glue on dried grass heads. Cover both sides of the cardstock with dried grasses to make a nice bushy tail.

5

Use a cool melt glue gun to stick the tail to the base of the cone, so it curves up over the body.

6

Glue two small dried leaves to the head for ears. Paint an acorn cup black and glue to the face to make a nose.

7

Cut out a pair of arms from thick cardstock and paint brown. Use the template on page 69 as a guide.

8

Glue the arms to the sides of the cone.

9

Glue on two shells for eyes. Add a dot of black paint to each one. Then give him a tasty nut for his dinner.

23

Butterflies

Choose clean feathers to make your butterfly wings. Smooth them with your fingers to rejoin any separated parts.

You will need

Feathers (from a store)
Cardstock
Acorn cups
Dried beans or peas
Short, thin sticks

1

Pair up the feathers to make a roughly symmetrical butterfly.

2

Try to use feathers with nice markings. Keep these natural and paint any plainer ones.

3

Cut out two body shapes from cardstock. Paint one of the pieces of cardstock green.

4

Cut off the quill ends from the feathers. Glue a pair of feathers to the unpainted piece of cardstock.

5

Add more feathers until you have a pair of colorful wings.

6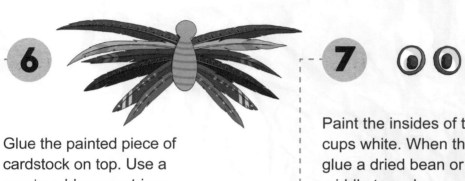

Glue the painted piece of cardstock on top. Use a pen to add some stripes.

7

Paint the insides of two acorn cups white. When they are dry, glue a dried bean or pea in the middle to make a pair of eyes.

8

Cut two short lengths of thin stick. If they are not too brittle, bend the ends over a little. These will be the antennae.

9

Glue the eyes to the front and the antennae to the back of the butterfly head. Add a smile!

FLUTTER

FLUTTER

FLUTTER

Trees

1 Cut the sticks so that each one is slightly longer than the previous one. You will need 10–14 sticks for one tree.

2 Paint some of the sticks green and leave others unpainted.

3 Paint the craft stick brown. Glue on the sticks to make a triangle—start with the shortest at the top and work down to the longest one..

4 Glue a loop of ribbon to the back.

5 Repeat steps 1–4 to make a multi-colored tree, too, and hang them to decorate your room.

Snowflake

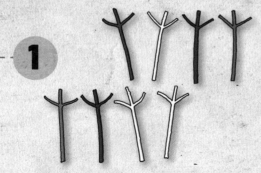

1 Cut the eight sticks roughly the same length. Paint them white.

You will need

Eight narrow sticks with side shoots

Thick cardstock

Dried spices

Stick-on sparkly gems

2 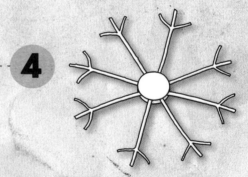 Cut out two circles from thick cardstock and paint white.

3  Glue the straight ends of the sticks onto one of the circles of cardstock.

4 Glue the other circle on top. Leave to dry.

5 Glue on some dried spices, such as star anise, cardamom, and cloves. Add sparkly gems to finish your winter decoration.

Spider and Web

Some spiders spin a silk web to catch insects for food. Others simply pounce on their prey.

1

Paint half a walnut shell black.

2

Cut each chenille stem into four pieces to make eight legs for your spider. Glue the legs to the inside of your shell, four on each side.

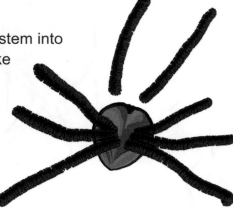

3

Turn your spider up the right way and bend its legs so it stands up.

4

Lay your twigs across one another as shown, tie them in the middle with a piece of yarn. This will be the base for the web.

5

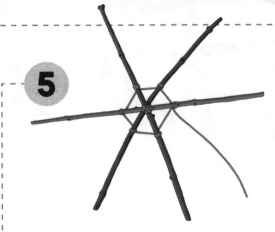

Cut a length of yarn and start tying it near the middle of the web. Wrap it around each stick in turn. When you get back to where you started, knot it and cut off any extra yarn.

6

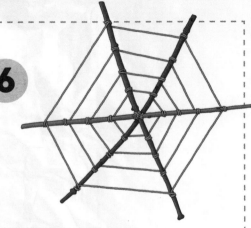

Repeat Step 5 three more times, moving outward from the center to make a large web for your spider.

7

Glue two lentil eyes to your spider and add a dot to each with a black pen. Attach the spider by bending its legs around the web so that it is ready to pounce!

Handy Hint

Spider webs are easiest to see on bushes on still fall mornings. Take a look at the intricate patterns of the webs and use them as inspiration when you make your web.

Mice

Mice range in color from white to dark brown, gray or black.

You will need

Whole nut shells
Pink felt
Dried beans
Dried lentils or peas

1

Paint your nut shells different shades of gray or leave them their natural color.

2

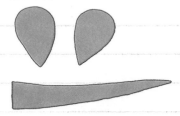

Cut out a tail and a pair of ears from pink felt for each mouse.

3

Glue the ears and tails to the mice.

4

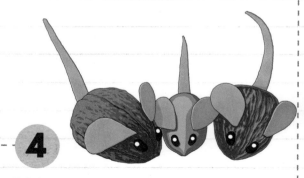

Stick on two beans for eyes to each mouse. Add a dot of white paint to the center of each one.

5

Glue on a dried lentil or pea to each mouse for a nose. The mice are ready to cause mischief!

squeak!

Penguins

Helicopter seeds are the seed pods from maple and sycamore trees. They spin as they fall from the trees.

1

Paint the rough stone white. Add a pale blue edge. This is your iceberg.

2

Paint a white oval on the front of each pebble. When dry, paint the rest of both pebbles black.

3

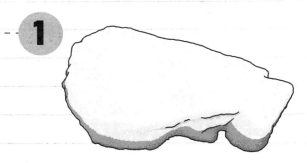

Paint two half pistachio nut shells yellow. Glue them onto each pebble for beaks. Glue on two dried peas for eyes and add a black dot to each.

4

Paint the helicopter seeds black and glue one pair to the back of each pebble for wings.

5

Use a cool melt glue gun or adhesive putty to stick the pebble penguins to the iceberg.

31

Sun Picture Frame

You will need

Thick cardstock
Lots of thin sticks
Dried beans of different colors
Ribbon

1 Cut out two circles from thick cardstock. Make sure one circle is very slightly smaller than the other. Cut out a circle from the middle of the largest circle.

2 Paint the large circle yellow. This will be the frame.

3 Glue four long sticks around the frame.

4 Glue on more sticks. Space them evenly around the frame. Paint the ends of the sticks yellow.

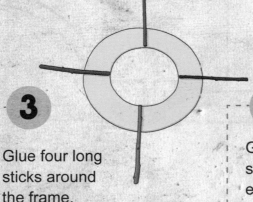

5 Put some glue into every other gap between the sticks. Place different colored dried beans onto the glue.

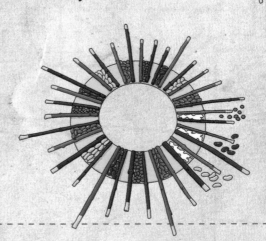

6

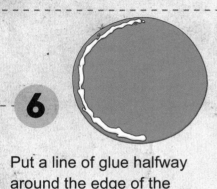

Put a line of glue halfway around the edge of the smaller circle.

7

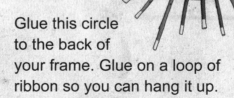

Glue this circle to the back of your frame. Glue on a loop of ribbon so you can hang it up.

8

The unglued section at the back means you can slide in your favorite picture to the frame.

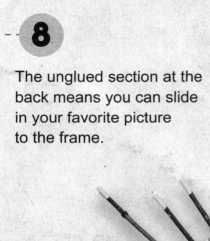

Reindeer

Reindeer live in cold places. They use their hooves to dig for food in the snow.

You will need

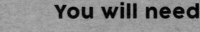

Two narrow logs, one thicker than the other

Saw (adult use)

Hand drill (adult help)

Five thin, straight sticks

Two thin sticks with side shoots

Acorn cup

Small cockle shell

Two dried beans

Two pistachio shells

1

Ask an adult to cut the thickest log with a saw to make the body. From the narrow log, cut a section about three-quarters the length of the body. This will be the head.

2

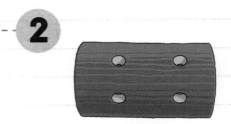

Get an adult to drill four holes in the body. They should be slightly bigger than your thin straight sticks and should be angled toward the middle of the body.

3

Turn the body over and drill another hole near one end. This should be angled toward the back of the body.

4

Cut four thin sticks the same length for the legs. Put a dab of glue into the four holes on the base of the body. Push the thin sticks into the holes.

5

Cut a thin stick shorter than the legs. Glue this into the top hole on the body to make a neck.

6

Take the head and drill a hole near one end. This should go straight down.

7

Turn the head over and drill two holes for the antlers. Make sure they are on the same end as the previous hole.

8

Glue the head onto the neck.

9

Glue the two sticks with side shoots into the holes. These are the antlers.

10

Stick on a pistachio shell for each ear. Paint an acorn cup black and glue on for the nose. Add two dried bean eyes and a cockle shell tail. Paint a white spot on each eye and add spots to the body and head.

Snake

You will need

Long, twisted stick
Yarn
Foam ball
Two small shells
Helicopter seed

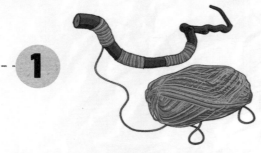

1

Wrap lengths of yarn around the stick. Either tie or glue it in place. Leave some sections of the stick unwrapped.

2

Paint a foam ball green to make the head. When dry, use the tip of a pencil to dig out a hole that is large enough to fit the thickest end of the stick.

3

Dab glue on the thick end of the stick and push on the head.

4

Glue on two shells for eyes. Paint a spot on each eye and add a few paint spots to the head.

5

Remove and discard the seed part of a helicopter seed. Paint the two pieces of the helicopter seed pink to make the tongue.

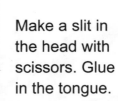

6

Make a slit in the head with scissors. Glue in the tongue.

crab

1

Paint six cockle shells bright orange.

2

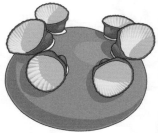

Paint the pebble pale orange. When dry, glue the cockle shells to the base for the feet.

3

Glue on two snail shells to the top of the pebble for eyes.

4

Glue two dried leaves to a piece of cardstock. Cut them out and then cut in half along the vein in the middle. Glue each one to a short, thin stick for claws.

5

Glue the claws to the top of the pebble. Paint on some yellow spots and add a smile. Look out for those pincers!

Tree Frogs

Tree frogs can be green, gray, or brown, or very brightly colored. They live in hot parts of the world.

You will need

Long, thin sticks with side shoots

Short, thin sticks with side shoots

Smooth pebbles

Acorn cups

Yellow cardstock

1

Cut two long, thin sticks with side shoots for the back legs. Carefully bend the sticks to the side about halfway along the stem. They may partially snap, which is fine.

2

Cut another two sticks with side shoots to make the front legs. These should be shorter than the back legs. Paint all the legs green, or leave natural.

3

Paint a pebble green or leave natural. Use a cool melt glue gun to attach the legs to the body.

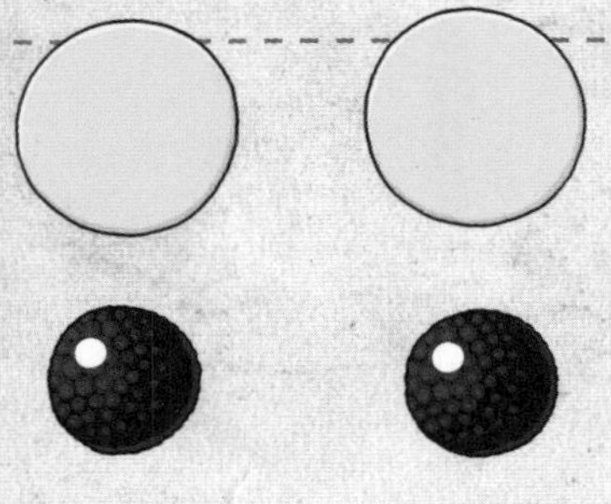

4

Paint two acorn cups black. Add a white dot to each. Cut out two circles from yellow cardstock. Make these slightly larger than the acorn cups.

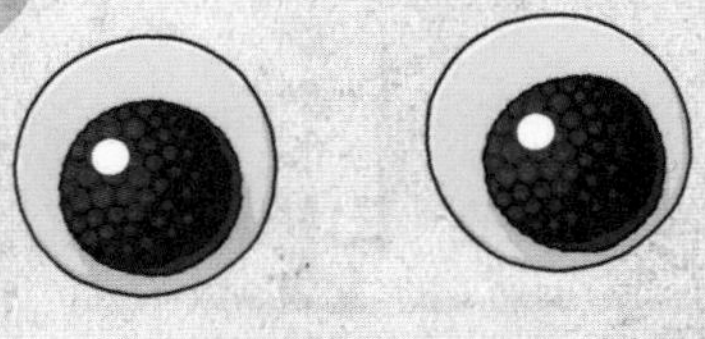

5

Glue the acorn cups to the circles to make the eyes.

6

Glue the eyes to the top of the body. Add some spots. Your frog is ready to hop off!

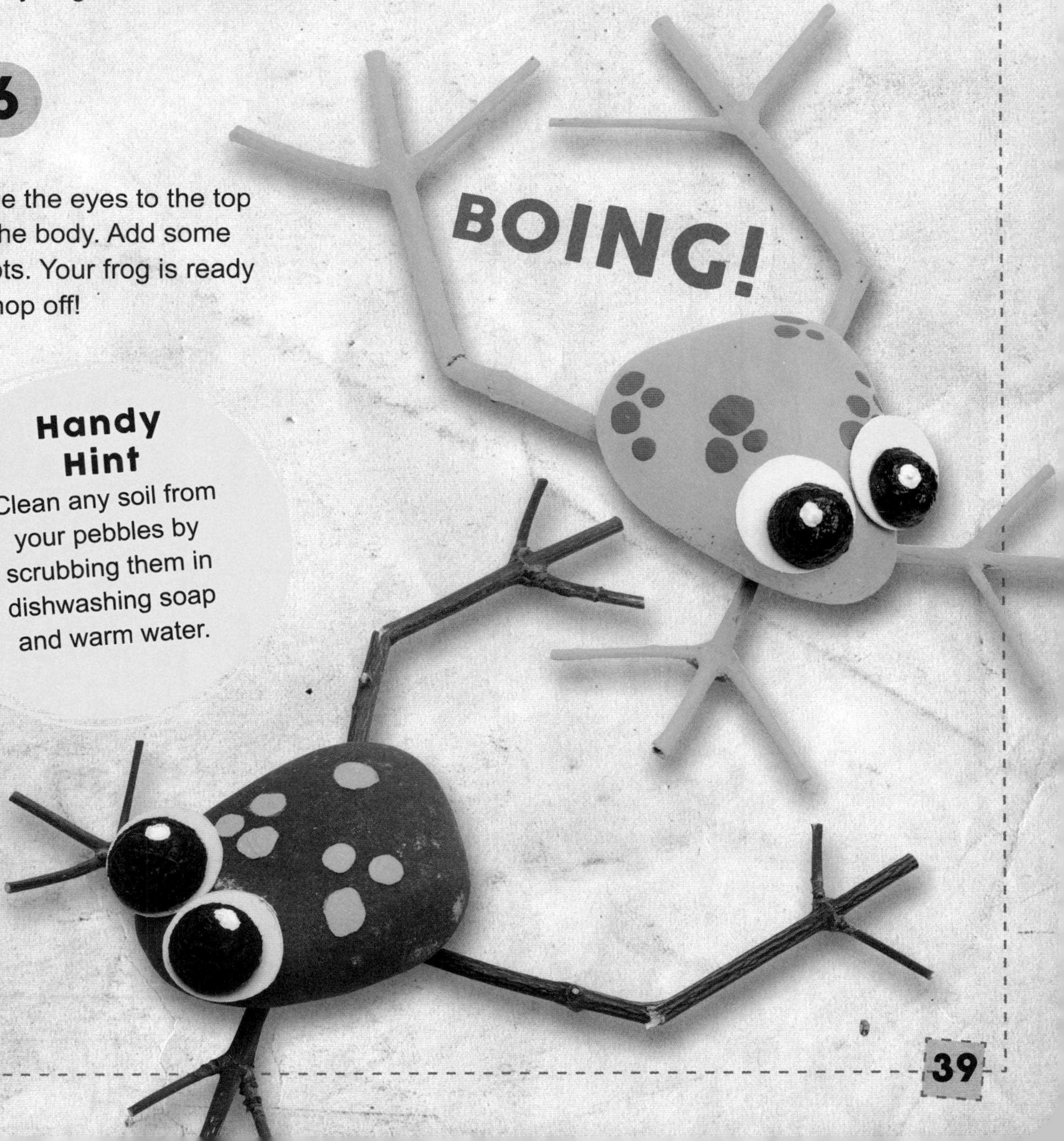

Handy Hint

Clean any soil from your pebbles by scrubbing them in dishwashing soap and warm water.

BOING!

Peacock

Male peacocks use their magnificent tail feathers to impress the females.

1

Paint the foam egg and the large pine cone blue. Glue the egg to the cone at an angle.

2

Place the two sticks with side shoots as shown.

3

Put some glue on the straight end of the sticks and place the large cone on top. You now have a peacock body and legs.

4

Paint the spiral seashell yellow. Gently twist the shell into the front of the head. Remove it, then glue in place.

5

Paint the ends of three small cones yellow.

6

Use the tip of a pencil to make three holes in the top of the head. Glue the small cones into the holes.

7

Cut out a triangle from thick cardstock and paint it blue.

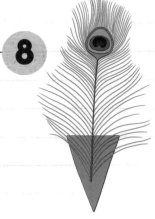

8

Glue a peacock feather to the cardstock. Make sure it is taller than your peacock's body.

Handy Hint

You can buy peacock feathers in craft shops and online.

9

Glue on more feathers to look like a fan. This is the tail.

10

Glue the tail to the back of the body. Add a pair of googly eyes and your peacock is ready to impress.

Lizard

Lizards are cold blooded. This means they need heat from the Sun to warm their bodies. Let your lizard bask on a warm windowsill.

1

Ask an adult to cut a section of the thick stick for the body. Paint the stick and the egg green. Glue the egg to the stick.

2

Cut two long, thin sticks with side shoots for the back legs. Carefully bend the sticks to the side about halfway along the stem.

3

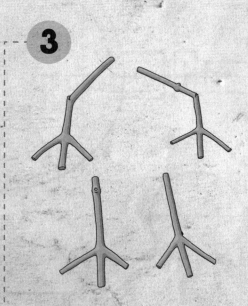

Cut another two sticks with side shoots. These need to be shorter than the back legs. Paint all the legs green.

4

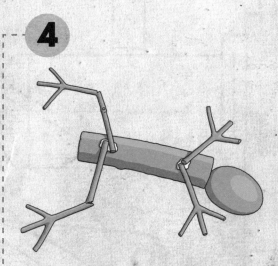

Use a cool melt glue gun to attach the legs to the body.

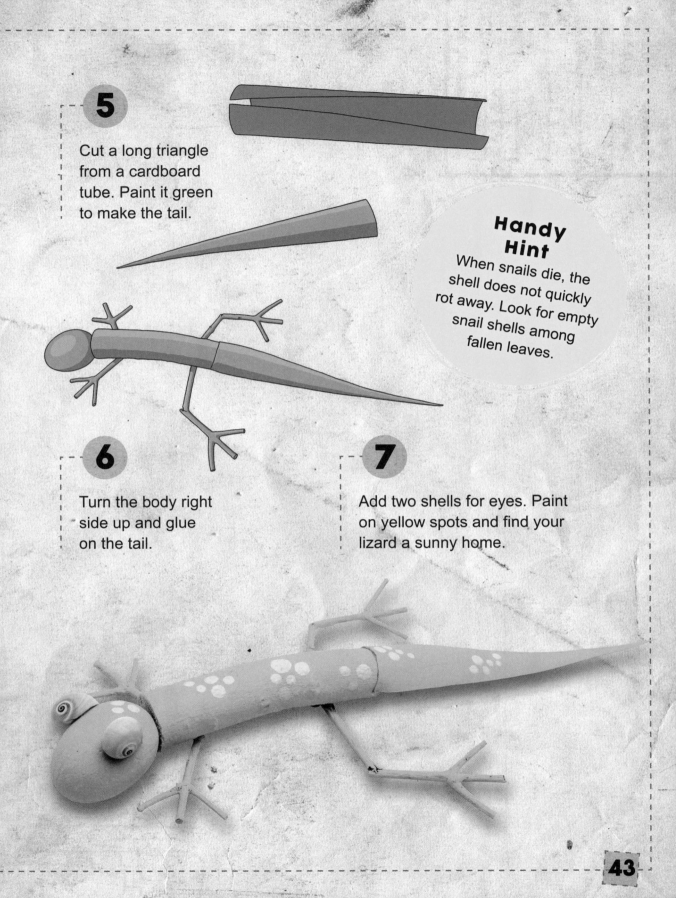

5

Cut a long triangle from a cardboard tube. Paint it green to make the tail.

Handy Hint

When snails die, the shell does not quickly rot away. Look for empty snail shells among fallen leaves.

6

Turn the body right side up and glue on the tail.

7

Add two shells for eyes. Paint on yellow spots and find your lizard a sunny home.

Caterpillars

Caterpillars eat and eat as they prepare to turn into a butterfly. During this time they shed their skin around five times.

1

Paint your bent sticks. These will be the bodies.

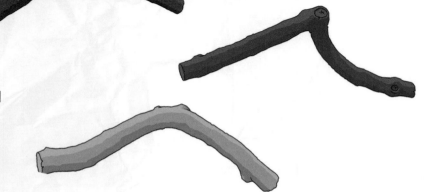

2

Paint the foam balls to match the bodies. These are the heads. Use the tip of a pencil to dig out a hole in each one, large enough to fit the bent stick.

3

Put a dab of glue on the end of the body sticks and push into each head. Wrap and glue on colored raffia around the bodies.

4

Make two small holes in the top of the head with a pencil. Put some glue on the end of two short sticks and push into the holes.

5

Paint large black dots in the middle of two acorn cups for each caterpillar. Add a small dot of white paint to each.

6

Glue the acorns to the front of the heads for eyes.

Handy Hint

If the caterpillars do not balance on the larger stick, use adhesive putty to keep them in place.

7

Put your caterpillars on the larger stick so they can make it their home.

Hedgehog

1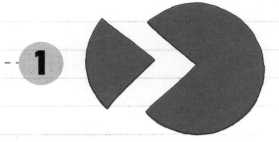

Cut out a circle from felt. Cut out a quarter section and keep it to make the ears later.

2

Twist the rest of the felt into a cone. Glue it in place.

3

Cut out a pair of ears from the leftover felt quarter.

4

Glue the ears to the inside of the felt cone.

5

Glue the felt cone to the top of the pine cone.

6

Paint an acorn cup black and glue to the tip of the felt cone for a nose. Glue on two dried beans for eyes. Paint a white dot onto each eye and your hedgehog is ready to scurry away.

Bugs

You will need

Two whole walnuts
Two cockle shells
Four dried lentils
Bark

1

Paint one walnut shell half red, half black for a ladybug. Paint the other walnut shell half yellow, half black for a bee.

2

Paint black stripes on the yellow part of the bee. For the ladybug, paint the narrow end black and add black spots to the rest of the body.

3

Glue on two small cockle shells to the bee for wings.

4

Stick dried lentils to each bug for eyes. Draw black dots on the lentil eyes and add a smile to the bee. Place the bugs on their woody home.

Handy Hint

If you cannot find bark for your bugs' home, a log would work well, too.

47

Puppets

Dry flowers for your puppets by pressing them between the pages of a heavy book.

1

Paint the poppy seed head any skin color. Glue the stem inside a paper straw.

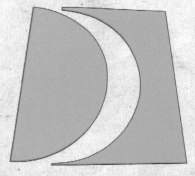

2

Cut out a semicircle from cardstock. Keep the offcuts for the arms.

3

Glue the semicircle of cardstock into a cone shape, leaving a small hole at the top. Use clothespins to hold in place while the glue dries.

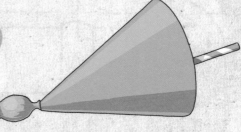

4

Slide the straw into the cone. Add a dab of glue to keep it in place.

5

Push cotton wool into the cone around the straw to keep it from moving.

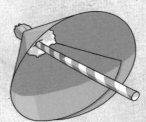

6

Cut out a pair of arms from the offcuts of cardstock. Glue on the sticks with side shoots to the top half of the arms. These are the hands. Fold the arms in half and glue to trap the hands inside.

7

Glue the arms to the back of the cone.

8

Add shells, helicopter seeds, and other seed pods to the head to make hair and features.

9

Add seed pods or dried flowers to the body.

10

Glue on googly eyes. Make more puppets using different seed pods and put on a show.

Koala

Koalas climb trees and eat eucalyptus leaves.

1

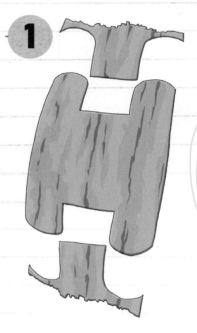

Handy Hint
Do not peel bark off living trees. Use a felled tree or look for bark that has already fallen off.

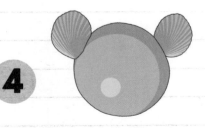

Flatten your piece of bark. Cut out an "H" shape. Use the template on page 70 as a guide. This will be the body.

2

Paint a cardboard tube gray. Glue the bark body around the tube, leaving the paws unglued. Use clothespins to hold it in place while it dries.

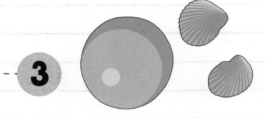

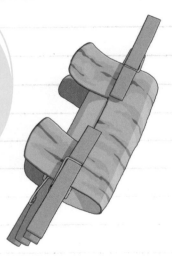

3

Paint the foam ball and two cockle shells gray. These will be the head and ears.

4

Make an indent with a pencil on either side of the ball. Glue the cockle shells into these indents.

5

Paint an acorn cup black. Glue two dried beans and the acorn cup on for a nose and eyes. Add a dot of white paint to each eye.

6

Glue the head to the body and stick on a cockle shell tail.

7

Cut out leaf shapes from green cardstock and glue them to the top of the short, thick stick. Glue your cute koala to the tree.

Crocodile

This crocodile has limpet shell scales. Do not take living limpet shells from rocks. Look for empty ones along the shore.

You will need

Two long cardboard tubes

Small log, about as thick as your wrist

Thick cardstock

Four scallop shells

About 20 small cockle shells

About 14 limpet shells

Two acorn cups

1

Cut one of the cardboard tubes along its length.

2

Paint the opened tube and the top of the log green. Glue the end of the open tube around one end of the log. Glue the other end of the tube into a cone shape.

3

Cut out four legs from thick cardstock—two short and two long ones. Use the templates on page 71 as a guide.

4

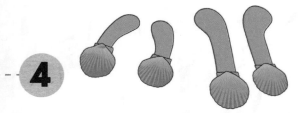

Glue a scallop shell to the end of each leg. Paint them all green.

5

Glue the legs to the log. Make sure the short ones are at the front.

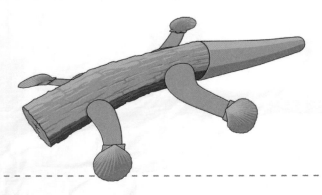

6

Cut the other cardboard tube along its length. Then cut into two pieces lengthways. You now have two jaws. Cut a section off one of the pieces to make it a little shorter. Paint the outsides of the tubes green and the insides dark pink.

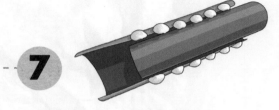

7

Glue cockle shells along the straight edges of the jaw tubes for teeth. It helps to use a spare tube to support the mouth while the glue dries.

8

Glue the short jaw to the bottom, and the long jaw to the top of the log.

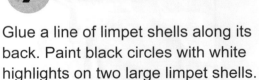

9

Glue a line of limpet shells along its back. Paint black circles with white highlights on two large limpet shells. Glue these to the top of the head.

10

Glue on two acorn cups for nostrils. Paint on some yellow spots and your crocodile is ready to go!

SNAP
SNAP

Lion Mask

Look for fallen leaves in fall. Press them flat inside a heavy book to dry. They will be ready to use after about a week.

You will need

Yellow cardstock

Plates and jars of different sizes

White cardstock

Thin elastic

Fallen leaves—yellow, gold, and brown

Black felt

1

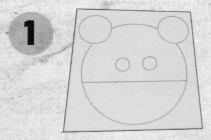

Draw around a plate (about 12 inches or 30 cm across) on yellow cardstock. Next, draw around a jar to make two ears. Add two circles in the middle for eyes. Draw a line below the eyes.

2

Cut out the mask. Use a pencil to make a hole for your scissors when you cut out the eyes. Paint the inside of the ears pink.

3

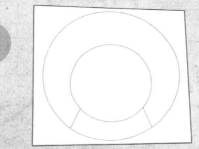

Draw a circle on white cardstock larger than the plate you used. Draw another circle inside it, making it smaller than the plate and off-center.

4

Cut out the circles and cut out a section from the bottom. Use the tip of a pencil to make a hole in both sides. Tie a piece of elastic through the holes.

5

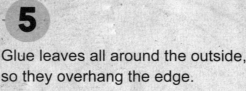

Glue leaves all around the outside, so they overhang the edge.

6

Continue with more leaves, overlapping them until you only have a small area of white cardstock showing.

7

Put some glue on the white areas of cardstock, then glue the yellow piece on top.

8

Cut out two round shapes of white cardstock. Glue to the bottom left and right of the mask.

9

Cut two leaves in half and glue above the eyes for eyebrows.

10

Cut out a nose from black felt and glue it on. Draw on some whiskers. Put on your mask and you are ready to roar!

Dinosaur

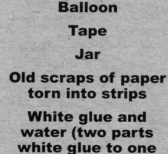

1 Blow up a balloon and tie the end. Use tape to attach it to a jar. Dip strips of newspaper into your glue mix and lay them on the balloon. Cover the top half of your balloon with three layers of paper.

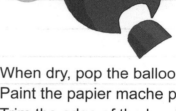

2 When dry, pop the balloon. Paint the papier mache purple. Trim the edge of the bowl shape and cut out a semicircle from the edge.

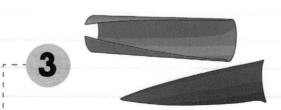

3 Cut out a long triangle from the cardboard tube. Paint it purple to make a tail.

4 Glue or tape the tail into the semicircle in the body.

5 Use the tip of a pencil to make holes along the middle of the body and tail. Glue short lengths of thin stick into the holes.

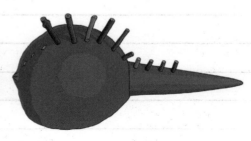

6

Make a hole with a pencil in the front end of the body. Then use scissors to cut slits out from the hole.

7

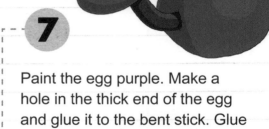

Paint the egg purple. Make a hole in the thick end of the egg and glue it to the bent stick. Glue the stick into the hole in the body.

8

Ask an adult to help cut four short lengths of a thick stick. Glue these to the inside edge of the body. Stuff the body with scrunched up newspaper to make it stronger.

9

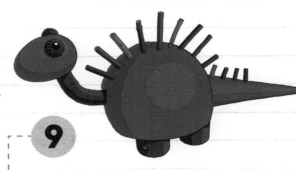

Paint black circles on two acorn cups. Add a white dot to each. Glue these eyes to the head.

ROARRR!
ROAR!

10

Paint on some yellow spots and your dinosaur is free to roam.

Angels

You will need

Glitter glue	Dried leaves
Pine cone	Glittery pipe cleaner
Foam ball	Dried lentils
Yarn	

1

Put some glitter glue onto the tips of the scales of a pine cone.

2

Paint the foam ball any skin color. Glue the ball to the top of the cone.

3

Cut some lengths of yarn and glue them to the top of the ball for hair.

4

Paint two dried leaves white and glue them to the back of the cone for wings.

5

Cut a pipe cleaner in half and twist it into a circle. Glue it to the back of the head for a halo.

6

Glue on some dried lentils for eyes, add a smile and rosy cheeks with a felt-tip pen, and your angel is ready to fly.

Parrot

You will need

Long pine cone
Mussel shells (one pair and one single)
Helicopter seed

Felt
Two googly eyes
Thick stick

1

Paint the pine cone red.

2

Paint a pair of mussel shells with a band of red, yellow, and blue. These are the wings.

3

Glue the wings to either side of the cone. Push them between the scales to hold them in place.

4

Paint a helicopter seed red. Cut it in half. These will make the tail.

5

Glue the tail to the narrow end of the cone.

6

Glue a single, unpainted mussel shell to the thick end of the cone to make a beak. Cut out two circles of felt and glue on googly eyes. Glue these to the cone. Find a stick for your parrot to perch on.

Sheep

In the winter when sheep have their full, fleecy coats, look for tufts of fleece caught on fences or bushes.

1

Ask an adult to help cut four short pieces of a thick stick. Glue these stick legs to a rectangle of thick cardstock.

2

Tie the pine cone to the cardstock with string. Wrap the string around the cone at least three times to make it secure.

3

Turn the model over so the legs are at the bottom. Paint the foam egg black. Glue it to the wide end of the cone.

4

Poke pieces of fleece into the gaps between the scales of the cone. Use a pencil to push it deep into the cone.

5

Continue covering the cone with fleece.

6

Make two small indents on the top of the head. Glue a mussel shell into each hole for ears.

7

Glue more fleece between the ears. Add two small shells for eyes and one for a nose. Add a black dot with a felt-tip pen onto each eye. Your sheep can now go off to graze.

Handy Hint
Put your fleece in a bowl filled with warm water and dishwashing soap. Let it soak for 30 minutes to remove any grease.

Mushrooms

You will need

Seven limpet shells
Thin, twisted sticks
Modeling clay
Thick stick
Hand drill (adult help)

1

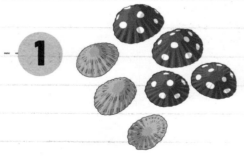

Paint some of the limpet shells red with white spots. Leave some shells their natural color.

2

Cut some thin, twisted sticks similar lengths to make the mushroom stems.

3

Push a piece of modeling clay into each shell. Push a stick stem into the clay.

4

On a thick stick, drill some holes that are slightly wider than the stick stems.

5

Add a dab of glue to each hole. Push in the mushroom stems. Your mushroom garden is complete.

Snowman

1

Paint a poppy seed head white and an acorn cup red.

You will need

One poppy seed head
One acorn cup
Foam ball
Two sticks with side shoots
Small red pompom
Ribbon
Dried lentils (or peppercorns)
Orange cardstock

2

Make a hole with the tip of a pencil in the foam ball. Push the poppy stem into the hole.

3

Use a pencil to make a hole on each side of the ball. Push a stick into each hole for the arms.

4

Glue the red acorn cup to the top of the poppy seed head. Glue on a red pompom. Tie a ribbon around its neck.

5

Glue on two lentils as eyes. Cut out a small triangle of orange cardstock and glue it on as a nose. Draw on a smile to finish your happy snowman.

63

Birds

Choose bright colors for your birds or try to re-create birds that you see outside your home.

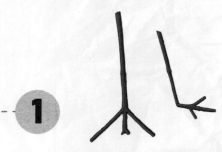

1 Cut two thin sticks with side shoots the same length. Carefully bend the sticks upward just above the side shoots to make them into feet.

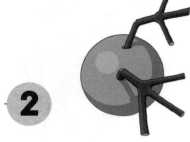

2 Paint the foam ball. Use the tip of a pencil to make two holes, close together, in the ball. Push the feet into the holes.

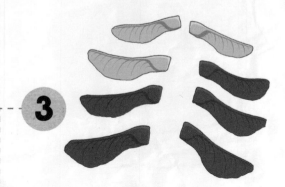

3 Cut four helicopter seed pairs in half. Paint them or leave a natural color.

4 Make a pair of wings by gluing together three of the half helicopter seeds as shown.

5 Glue the wings to each side of the ball.

6 Make a tail with the remaining two half helicopter seeds.

7

Cut a slit in the back of the ball. Put glue onto the narrow part of the tail and push into the slit.

8

Paint half a pistachio nut shell yellow. Push the edge of it into the front of the ball. Remove it and add a dab of glue before pushing it back into place.

9

Add a pair of dried bean eyes. Follow the steps again to make a flock of birds.

Handy Hint

If your birds will not stand up, press their feet into small pieces of adhesive putty.

Cacti

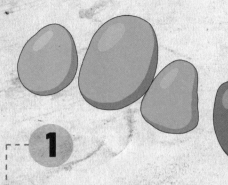

1

Paint your pebbles different shades of green.

2

Add some detail, such as spots or stars, to look like spikes.

3

Paint some beechnuts to look like flowers.

4

Put dry sand or gravel into a flower pot. If your pot has a hole in the bottom, cover it with tape first.

5

Push your pebble cacti into the gravel. Then glue on your flowers to create a beautiful display.

Chicken and Chicks

You will need

Foam egg	Thin sticks with side shoots
Half coconut shell	Googly eyes
Three pairs of mussel shells	Dried beans
Beechnut	Dried lentils (or peppercorns)
Pistachio nut shell	
Whole walnuts	

1

Paint the foam egg brown. When dry, glue it to the coconut shell for a head.

2

Glue a pair of mussel shells to each side of the coconut shell. Glue another pair to the back. These are the wings and tail.

3

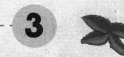

Paint a beechnut red.

4

Make a hole with a pencil in the top of the head. Glue the beechnut into the hole. Paint a half pistachio nut shell yellow. Glue it to the front of the head.

5

Paint a walnut yellow. This will be a chick. Glue the two sticks with side shoots to the base for feet.

6

Glue on a pair of googly eyes to the chicken and the chick. Glue on a dried bean to the chick for a beak. Make another chick to sit with the hen.

Templates

Bird Mask Template
(Pages 8–9)

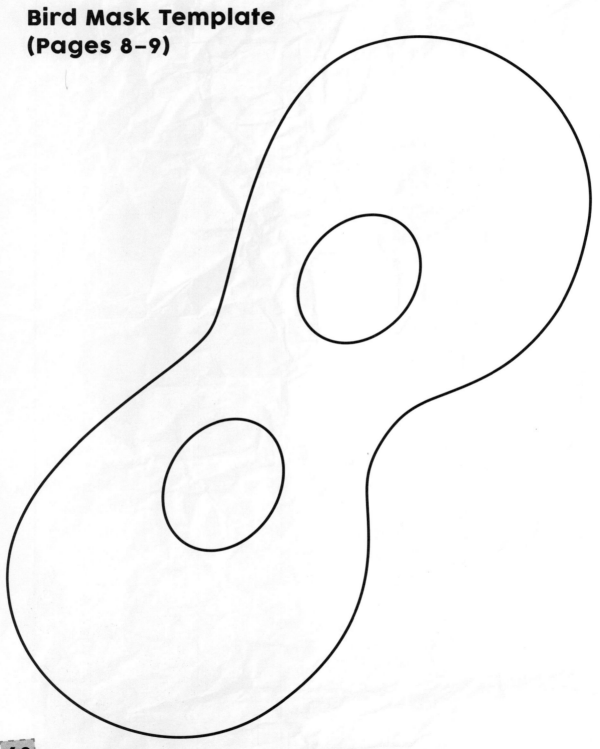

Flower Petal Template
(Page 11)

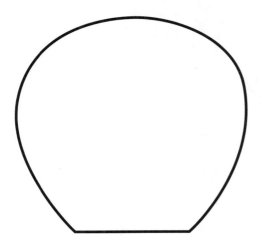

Squirrel Arms Template
(Pages 22–23)

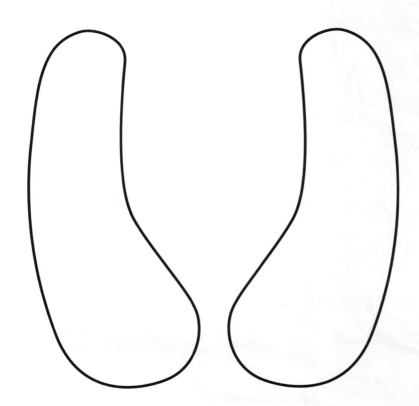

Koala Body Template
(Pages 50–51)

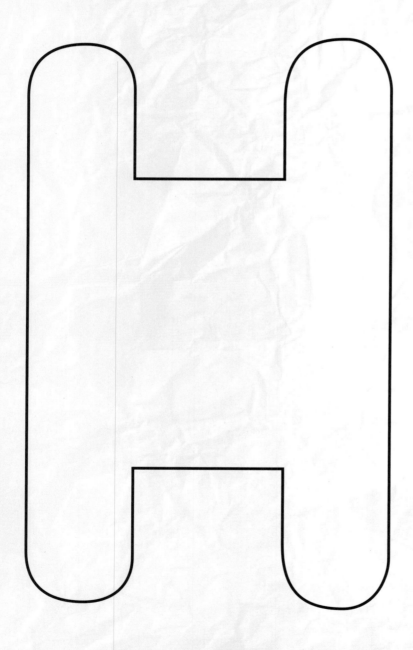

Crocodile Leg Template
(Pages 52–53)

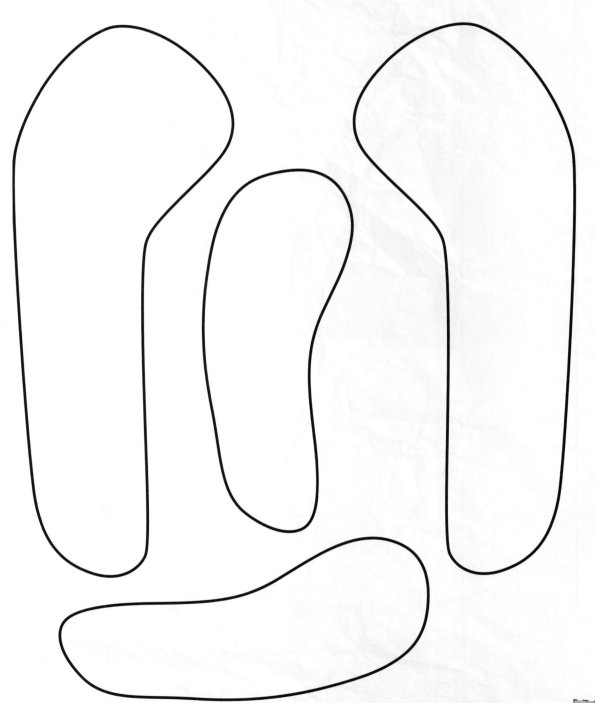

Nature Craft Tips

Which natural materials do you need?

Take a look at the projects you want to make.
List or sketch the materials you need to find.

Which natural materials have you found?

List or sketch your finds here.

Where will you look for your materials?

List the places you will visit to find your materials and sketch the trees, plants, and items you want to find.

Have you thought about...?

Think about what else you will need to take on your hunt—a bucket, a spade, a bag? Will you need an adult with you when you hunt for your natural materials? Make a list.

Nature box

Keep your finds safe in a nature box. Use some of your natural materials to decorate a cardboard box. Divide the box into sections with strips of cardstock, so you can organize what you have collected. List or draw the items you'd like to collect for your dream nature box.

Shell logbook

Sketch or draw around any shells that you have collected.

Pressed leaf pictures

Use this page to sketch your favorite wildlife. Now use pressed leaves to create these animals by gluing them onto paper. Try a fox, an owl, or a hedgehog.

Rubbings

Use natural materials to create rubbings. Place a thin sheet of paper over the veined side of a leaf or bark. Rub a wax crayon across the paper and over the material. Try different textures and colored crayons. Create a collage of them on this page.